The Fool's Inkwell

Edwin Espinel

BookLeaf Publishing

India | USA | UK

Presentation by *BookLeaf Publishing*

Web: www.bookleafpub.com

E-mail: info@bookleafpub.com

ISBN: 9789358311266

First edition 2023

ACKNOWLEDGEMENT

I would like to acknowledge the following people that have helped me throughout my life to get to this point.

Dilan "Dippy" Alpay
Kevin Gubelman

And many of the people who have read and been moved by my poetry. Thank you very much. Without your help or appreciation these poems would have never come to light.

PREFACE

I am Edwin Espinel a first generation American; and all around bard. This a compilation of poems that I have decided to take the challenge for. This book is made throughout July. I will be filling it with poems throughout my adventures in that month. Hopefully it is enjoyable or at least can help those that need it.

Am I Icarus

The question that comes to my mind is what was
in the head of the one who fell
The one who trusted so much but listened so
little
We hear of his legend and how he did not heed a
warning
But how can one hear when the air rushes so fast
that everything else is deafened
Was it hubris or was it love of life?
To caress the sky and be burned by the sun
A lesson is learned through blood and tears
But was immortalized for years and years
So is the story of icarus a cautionary tale?
Or is it one that tells us that we should let our
wings sail

Somewhere Else

In another life
In another time
I hold you close
But not because you are mine

It is for you tug at my heart strings
Know every word to put me to heel
And if you say yes
Then my secrets would be revealed
You would know of every thought that crossed
my mind
All you would have to do is ask

But sadly that world
Will most likely never
Come to pass
At least not in this space
Not in this time
Because I tried my best

But failed
Killing my heart
With promises of a life
That were only smoke and mirrors
By an illusionists designs

I see too much
Speak too little
But at the end of the day
Can not change the course
Of a life lived too minuscule

To only have memories strewn about
Like clutter in the mind
I should truly
Air them out
And stop wasting time

Be rid of the old
And in with the new
But I have so little left
Without the memories of all of you

Lucky charm

I am a lucky charm
When I leave
There will be no alarm

Merely a sense of peace
A breath of fresh air
As I go to my next affair

I leave a piece of myself everywhere I go
None will notice…
But their fortunes tends to turn

They believe that I am at peace
With a smile on my face
I am released

To go wherever "I" please
But no one checks
And often forget
The lucky charm
That is often left
Alone

Moored

There is true beauty in life
I know that it is there
I see it in the screens that are shown everywhere

I wish to touch the very images
That pop up and dazzle me

But they seem not to care
For the experience always passes me

I sit alone
In my room
Not knowing what to do
So I send off these messages
In hopes to find someone true

I am rutted in place
Needing a little help
That seems not to come…

At least thats what I tell myself
But these messages in bottles
Seem to surround me

I hope one day
That they can set me free
For while life may seem to be
A waiting game made to trap
Know that with a little help
The chains can be unwrapped

It takes a village

To those that do not know
A village must take care of their own
It is not only the children that need the help
It is the elders that can truly spread the wealth
Their knowledge can teach all that will listen
But watch as their eyes do glisten
With every tale that they spin
It is us who truly win
For their stories are worth more than gold
As long as we give them the time to be told

Insanity

By definition insanity is doing the same thing
and expecting a different result

But if practice makes perfect
Than does that not mean perfection is insane?
And if we follow that train of thought then what
is madness?
If not the pursuit of a perfection that may never
come!
A sorrow so deep
That can be described as a strange mood
For if we become passionate about something…
Then does that turn to insanity?
I for one embrace the chaos that comes from it
For creation is beauty
And to strive for an unattainable feat
In itself; is that not seraphic
A pursuit we will never obtain
But what we leave behind
Creates a paradise for those that need it
And cherished
By those who remain

Birthdays

I miss my past
Every year moves far too fast…
And yet when my birthday comes
It is never a celebration
It is a day of mourning;
Of remembering who no longer is there!
It's far too quiet…
We only eat in relative silence
The days of jubilation are gone
And all that is left is my lament

There is no fairness in it
Why do I get to age when they do not
And further why am I made to feel
As a wretch upon the celebration of my life
Perhaps because my life ended long ago…
Happy birthday to me?
My apologies…

Gauntlet

From my first breath
There has always been expectations
To do better
Go farther
But never to just be
You tell me now
Of how I was so perfect as a child
Never talked back
Never fought with you
But have you ever thought
Of why?

I was young
Had no knowledge of the world
You were supposed to teach
But you were not there long enough
Their is pain in my very dna
My blood pumps glass
Every single day

I remember the times you mention
Where I was good by your selection
By the reinforcing hand you would swing
Would catch me

But you never meant a thing
By the pain that you would bring
Upon the child
Who you sang to the heavens
You loved more than the world

But thats because the world hurt you more
Than I could ever understand
So you fed me rage
Taught me pain
And allowed me to drink of your tears

This is all I knew for years
Finally I ventured to learn
But could never leave this broken home
A bird with broken wings
Who dreamt past the gilded cage

I wonder why
He never speaks the same
After the gauntlet
In which he remains…

Moon

I look to the sky
so many times...

But it only feels right
When I see it at night
To look upon the moon
May bring out the mood
Of hope that hits my heart
Whenever we are apart

It is said that the moon brings out lunacy
For in its very name of luna that makes me see
How poets and romantics
Look up at the night sky
Wishing upon stars that they see past midnight
Hoping beyond all else to see the faces
That make them write
I too wish for that feeling
Would be for me

Strawberry

The taste on my lips
Lasts longer than I wish it did
The sweetness of strawberry
Remains in my mind
Haunts me from time to time

I live my life disoriented
Drunk on the sweetness
Without even drinking a single glass
I miss the summer days
Where the taste would last

But I live in my winter
Colder as each day passes
Fruits are sadly not as ripe
And the taste never…
Seems to keep

Still I will try to wander
To find the strawberry
That tasted of summer
Within my winter
Where I am sober

Universe

Why?

This place is so wide and expansive
Yet so small...

Although never small enough
Always a hurdle to climb
Another task to complete
But never can we just be…

They say the universe is both ever expanding
Yet there will be an end
Why then were we put here
To see a world die?

Because it has!
So many times…

Every flicker of light that falls from someones
eyes

I have seen the universe die
Explode into nothingness
And in my mind I scream

Louder and harder than any sound could truly
carry

For the screams in the mind pain me so
 I have seen cruelty
Both from familiar and unfamiliar alike
Yet I wish only…
To just be!

How sweet
To drift
And become nothing more than
Stardust…

Pencil

I often write not in pencil or pen
But digitally in the clouds
Where I can find more friends

I have tried to create
Through mediums that would stay
With ink that may stain
My hands once again

But it comes as a shock
How hard it becomes
To let go of things
That I create

Because ink may fade
And pencil erased
By those that think my art
Is nothing but common place

But at least in the clouds
I may save myself time
To write once again
And share with you my rhymes

Freezing

The cold bites at my face
As all I feel is rage
But the heat of it dies
As I look deep
Inside me
of all the things that reside

I wish I could tell
But the feeling
I am left with
is colder than hell

For your betrayal
stained my skin
Along with your every sin
But to hate you
Means you win

So I shall not give
That release that you so ask
To release us of the binds
That would let you win

For my hate for you
Has unshackled something deeper

For my hate for myself
Now waivers
With your favor

So thank you
For your cruelty
Has made me savor
The thought of living
Far past the life
That you never favored

Live?

The pain rushes to my chest
My heart begins to break
My veins boil
Wishing to burst and let me be free

But then you ask me
Something that slaps me awake
Your words sincere
Yet cursed just the same

You ask me to live…
How could you?
I have told you only a pittance
Of my past
And how it cycles
Too fast to break
And too strong to unravel

Yet you beg me softly
To survive…

My insides begin to churn…
Why should I?
You would bewitch me to stay
Force me to continue?!?

Every single day
Raked across the coals
Belittled battered and under minded…

It is good I have such hard skin
With a constitution to boot

So the scars do not last
But the ones that are "only" mental
Seem to shine so very bright

But no one can be there
For within my ornate cage
Few may tread
I grow lonelier by the day

But why should I bother you
With the details I so rue

…I guess at the end I will bid you
A mournful adieu…

Bells

I have never heard bells toll like these
When I was a child
they would sing merrily
For celebrations
Their song was so beautiful

Yet now it breaks my heart
For they do not toll for me
But for those that have known me
I am unable to see them

And yet they hold a death grip
On my heart
Every memory shatters me
I am the only one
who can pick up the pieces

Yet is it right
To even now
As I enter these church doors
Mourn a piece of me
That dies with thee

How the chimes
Will forever ring

through my soul
To a story
That has yet been told

Headspace

Every thought that races through my head
Creates so many images…
Some enlightening and inspiring!
While others are dreadful and send me
spiraling…

But I must pick and choose my battles
As I have been told many times before
For if I let myself think too much…
Their may be something to explore.
"Keep your head down!"
"Speak only when spoken to"
"Do not think when you are alone!"
For that is the time
Where the concept of freedom is explored!

The thunder of thought cracks in my mind
Making me think most of the time…

Music muffles and tv distracts
The screen time I take helps me "relax"
Consuming media in all its forms
Both muddles my mind but can sharpen it once
more…

Ramblings of the mad
Can be heard inside my dome
But I can never speak of it out loud
For no place is truly home…

Sure I had confidants once or twice
But it proved to be too much…
And they left or revoked the gift
Of listening to my strife

While I can fill so many cups with my misery
It seems like my happiness has always been near
empty

But I go on
Like a car on flat tires
Swerving on an empty road;
With no place to go
Or even rest…

For the next good mechanic
Is too far away
At best…

Self destruction

The feeling in the pit of my stomach
Like lava that boils me from the inside
But never to be let out
In fear of harming another

So I drown upon my own emotions
Silently let myself be overwhelmed
By voices that are not fully mine

In fact!
I barely recognize them
Perhaps it is my mind that has broken
Or in some way been opened
If only it was in the physical

But alas I can not say
Anything that races in my head as I stray
Or else I risk being put away
To be reprogrammed and reprimanded!

How dare I feel…
A travesty to think beyond my station
I am meant to be never heard
And barely seen

On a good day I disappear
But damn me for coming back.
I have no scars for I heal too quick
At least not any that can be tracked

With every quip I make there is a shutter
What if I hurt another?
Will I be thrown away?
Again…

For my value is nothing more than "friend"
A word that everyone uses
But never gives the life it deserves
Now meaning something akin to
Barely acquaintance
What does all this rambling mean?

Nothing
Which
Is all I am…

Agape

I yearn to love like the movies
To write stories of the countless times
I look in your eyes

A blessing to see your smile
And worship at your alter
With simple offerings
Such as breakfast in bed

Poems when you are too in your head
Songs that will stay in your heart
Music which makes the world fall apart
It would be a blessing to know what is in your
mind

Something I cherish
Is when I am given a moment of your time
These thoughts and memories
Will be kept in a box
Opened every time
I need a pick me up
Love is not a word strong enough
For how I feel makes the gods blush
So for you
The word agape must do…

A selfless love
That usually only gods know
May you be my blessing
Forever more

Gambit

Many say the mind is a terrible thing to lose
But what happens once it has gone?

Left entirely for something new
A perception of the world
That many would say is skewed

But the gambit that I take
Is that once your mind breaks
You can truly finally see
How the world is affected
By everything in ways
That none believe

As my heart trembles
And my excitement races
They call this mania
In that terrible place!

But is it not the love of life?
That has me in this state
The euphoria of living
In this maddened place
I can breath and sense the chemicals
In which make me, me!

But "Doctors" tend to disagree

There is a pill to make you slower
And ten more to chase the side effects
But this is no way to live…
By addling the mind
To mold how they think you should be

I know medicine is not to harm
But it does put me at alarm
When a diagnosis…
Becomes a blanket statement
For everything that "may" be wrong

So who is to say I am not right
When in the dark
The world shines so bright…

But I guess that is just a delusion
That helps me sleep
In my cold and restless nights.
As I lie in these sheets…

What if?

If I died today
But no one knew
How long would it take
For someone to find out?

I hermit often
For it is easier
Than to be with others
To have a chance to sour a relationship
No matter how small

I think of my transgressions
They overflow in my head
No matter how tiny they may be
My mind fosters them
And treats good thoughts as weeds
To be merely plucked out

So what if?
I think
When I truly wish to shout!
What if they knew
Of the time of my death?
It is not hard to see
That I have little time left…

Perhaps a few years
That go by in a flash
But I know; my impression wont last…

Merely another drop in the bucket
Of an uncaring place
I wish I was more selfish
To take a little more space
Than the scraps that were left over
And fallen to the floor
Not a moment was given
To make me feel more
So what would you do?

If I solemnly disappeared
Without a single word
And no chance
To reappear

Ghost of Icarus

Do not mourn me
For there is nothing to mourn for
Tis sad that life was lost this day
But knowledge was gained!

Oh father who crafts miracles
Shed no tears for me
For I shall shed more for you who is shackled
still to this world

Where there be cruelties abound
Although I did not see it with mine eyes
I know you have felt that cruelty in your heart
before
I; destined to be a martyr
To become legend and stand with you forever
more
My name, to live in immortality!
As a lesson to those who wish for more
But you did not feel the freedom
That you gifted
Only the consequences…

But had you known my bliss
Before the fall

I believe you would know
That it was worth it all.

www.ingramcontent.com/pod-product-compliance
Lightning Source LLC
Chambersburg PA
CBHW070614160726
48003CB00005B/2273